WHY WE TRAVEL

PATRICIA SCHULTZ

WORKMAN PUBLISHING • NEW YORK

*To Nick, who didn't know what he signed up for when he met me,
but who continues to embrace the journey—detours, potholes, and all.*

*To Roz and Ed and my whole family, who remind me that if not for home,
travel would bring me far less joy.*

*And everlasting thanks to my parents, who launched me on my quest to see the world
with our annual outings to the Jersey Shore, and who never once thought my dreams were too big.*

———————

"Passports to Understanding" from *Wouldn't Take Nothing for My Journey Now* by Maya Angelou. Copyright © 1993 by Maya Angelou.
Used by permission of Random House, an imprint and division of Penguin Random House LLC. All rights reserved.

A-You're Adorable Words and Music by Buddy Kaye, Sidney Lippman and Fred Wise.
Copyright © 1948, 1949 Sony Music Publishing (US) LLC and Aria Music. Copyrights Renewed.
All Rights on behalf of Sony Music Publishing (US) LLC Administered by Sony Music Publishing (US) LLC, 424 Church Street, Suite 1200, Nashville, TN 37219.
International Copyright Secured All Rights Reserved Reprinted by Permission of Hal Leonard LLC.

Library of Congress Cataloging-in-Publication Data is available.

ISBN 978-1-5235-1097-9

Jacket design by Vaughn Andrews
Interior design by Lisa Hollander
Photo Editor: Anne Kerman
Jacket photo by Martin Puddy/Stone/Getty Images
Title page photo by Ketkarn Sakultap/Moment/Getty Images

Workman books are available at special discounts when purchased in bulk for premiums and sales promotions as well as for fundraising or educational use.
Special editions or book excerpts can also be created to specification. For details, contact the Special Sales Director at specialmarkets@workman.com.

Workman Publishing Co., Inc.
225 Varick Street
New York, NY 10014-4381
workman.com

WORKMAN is a registered trademark of Workman Publishing Co., Inc.

Printed in South Korea on responsibly sourced paper
First printing August 2022

10 9 8 7 6 5 4 3 2 1

Travel is food for the soul.

experienced this epiphany at an early age. In fact, my earliest memory is not of my first bike or my first visit with Santa; it is of the morning we set off from my small hometown of Beacon in New York's Hudson Valley to Atlantic City and the Jersey Shore. I was four years old, sitting in the back seat of the family station wagon with my sister, Roz, the window rolled down and the wind on my face. I felt like the luckiest kid on the block. I loved the sound and smell of the ocean, the comical dive-bombing seagulls, and the long, sandy stretch of beach that beckoned me with the promise of the unknown. One day I wandered off alone just far enough for my mother to call the lifeguards into action. I was quickly found, though I never really considered myself lost. I remember how I did not want our summer adventure to end, and on our last day stood outside the car in a histrionic display of I-don't-want-to-go-home tears. It would be the first of many times I felt that way.

And just like that, Beacon was in my rearview mirror, and I was off to our nation's capital and a collegiate chapter that felt both exhilarating and enlightening.

My senior year saw everyone busy making plans for life after graduation—pursuing master's degrees, taking up the family business, or interviewing on Wall Street. With no real career plan in mind, I accepted my diploma, grabbed my passport, and set off for a gap year—which quickly turned from singular to plural—in Italy. A stint as a nanny for a dysfunctional but charming Florentine family, with two precocious children who forced me to learn Italian very quickly, led to gigs as a tour guide, translator, leather goods salesperson, and instructor of TEFL (teaching English as a foreign language). As a base, it allowed me to seek out relatives in my mother's ancestral hometown in Abruzzo, where, during my first visit, the town cobbler, a relative, proudly paraded me through town calling to his friends, *"Cugina d'America!"*—our American cousin!—

and brought me home to meet his young daughter, Patrizia, whom they had named after me. It was also a gateway to explore every corner of the country and much of Europe and northern Africa. I gained a different perspective on the United States and learned much about myself and what I valued—and I glimpsed the possibilities my future offered.

I realized that travel needed to play a big role in my life—though it would take me a while to figure out how. I am not one to count countries, but I can say I have seen more than that college graduate ever imagined.

As a twentysomething back home, between travels and still unsure of my path, I dabbled as a freelance fashion stylist. During a shoot in Key West for an Italian men's magazine, the editor was suddenly called back to Milan; with few options, he asked me to do a scheduled interview with a local personality—an eccentric sunken-treasure hunter of considerable fame. At that time, I was a master of postcard writing and not much else, but I accepted the assignment. Thankfully the treasure hunter loved to talk about himself—a lot—and gave me plenty of material to write the piece. What a thrill when I finally saw that first article published and my name in print! Proud and encouraged, I would spend the next many years blazing this new trail and saying yes to just about any assignment I was offered. It wasn't always easy, but it was always rewarding. And now, one thousand places later, I'm still at it and thankful every day.

Travel teaches us empathy, humility, patience, gratitude, and how to enjoy experiences over things; it is the ultimate classroom without walls. But travel is also just plain *fun*. It's a chance to cut loose, leave all the real-world stuff behind, and tap into your inner adventure seeker. On a recent trip to Southeast Asia, Elizabeth—a favorite traveling mate—and I were sailing down the Mekong River in Laos, and I felt a wave of contentment wash over me that I rarely feel at home. I felt both recharged and serene as we drifted through the legendary Golden Triangle, past scenery unchanged for centuries, a local captain at the helm of our polished wooden longboat. Children washing the family elephant on the sandy banks waved us on, their smiles contagious, while golden temples peeked out from densely forested hilltops. We stopped to visit villages stuck in time, explored a cave that had been transformed into a Buddhist temple filled with hundreds of statues, cooled off in hidden multitiered waterfalls, and eventually disembarked in Luang Prabang, a city whose name will always make me smile. Sometimes it is about both the journey and the destination.

Wherever you go, however you travel, allow it to enrich you, connect you to others, challenge your preconceptions, and open your head and heart. If you do, you'll understand why we travel, and why we should never stop. It is an investment in ourselves and makes us better people. When we get home, home is still the same, but we have changed. And that changes everything.

It's your road,
and yours alone.
Others may walk
it with you,
but no one can
walk it for you.

—RUMI

Left: Novice monk, Myanmar
Right: Umbrellas, Chiang Mai, Thailand

The first step . . .
shall be to lose
the way.

—GALWAY KINNELL

Left: Karnak Temple, Luxor, Egypt
Right: The Treasury, Petra, Jordan

Adventure nurtures lifelong friendships.

Left: Michelangelo's *David*
Right: Reflection of Ponte Vecchio in the Arno River, Florence

I had champagne taste and a house-wine budget when looking for a place to live in Florence during my post-collegiate days. I found the perfect spot: a rambling apartment in an old palazzo in the shadow of the Duomo. There was only one bed available and it was in a double room that I'd be sharing with another young woman. Flora, who turned out to be from New Jersey, hesitantly admitted she had hoped for an Italian-speaking roommate, and I confessed I had, too. But we embraced our avventura as innocents abroad, learning to bargain with the vendors at the Mercato Sant'Ambrogio, tirelessly sampling cafés in quest of the best cappuccino, sharing many a disastrous double date with local Casanovas, and escaping the days' heat at every free church concert we could find. Those ten months bonded us for life—and we have stayed BFFs ever since. Amiche per sempre!

I prefer
living in color.

—DAVID HOCKNEY

Left: Guanajuato, Mexico
Right: Painted door, Provence, France

Traveling—
it leaves you
speechless,
then turns you into
a storyteller.

—IBN BATTUTA

Zion National Park, Utah, USA

Use what you have.

From a display of umpteen shades—a veritable palette of India's many moods—and varieties of weight and quality, I finally chose a pashmina shawl, a little bit out of guilt, having occupied the patient but eager owner of the small shop in Rajasthan for many hours. It was the same terra-cotta rose that gave Jaipur the nickname the "Pink City." In 1876, Jaipur was painted this hue, a symbol of hospitality in Indian culture, to welcome the future king and emperor of India, Prince Albert Edward. I'm so glad I splurged on that purchase, as it has come to the rescue countless times over the years, pitching in as a layer against freezing planes, serving as a rolled-up head rest on long bus rides, adding a dash of elegance for that fancy dinner, and waiting in my bag to pinch-hit as a shoulder or head covering for unexpected visits to temples or mosques. I've even used it as a pillowcase substitute at a not-so-clean hotel—guaranteeing a good night's sleep and an occasional dream of faraway India.

Left: Rajasthani wall hanging
Right: Sari market, Rajasthan, India

Left: Serengeti
National Park,
Tanzania
Facing page:
Lion cub, Botswana

Be careful going in search of adventure—
it's ridiculously easy to find.

—WILLIAM LEAST HEAT-MOON

Embrace the challenge!

THERE'S NOTHING QUITE LIKE THE SATISFACTION of meeting a challenge head-on and rising to the occasion. Here are a few ways to test your mettle.

CONQUER A CITY. Exploring a metropolis like Tokyo or New York City can be downright intimidating, but when you seek out its less touristy corners, you'll understand its more authentic soul. One way to tap into the local scene is to use mass transit. Apps can make them easier to navigate and worth the effort. Once you do get the hang of the systems, you'll find them efficient and well organized—and fellow straphangers are surprisingly happy to help.

LEARN A FOREIGN LANGUAGE. Knowing another language will open up your world in countless ways and deepen your connection with others—whether you're bargaining at the market or bantering with a barista—while stretching your brain. Find an app or an online program and pair that with a language partner. It's also fun to immerse yourself in foreign films and books with easy story lines.

CLIMB A MOUNTAIN. Of the earth's various peaks, many require technical skill and experience to climb, but many others don't. Explore Mount Temple in Canada's beautiful Banff National Park (11,600 feet) and Mauna Kea in Hawaii, whose height is technically 33,500 feet, but more than half of that is submerged, making the above-sea-level mountain hikeable in four to five hours. Choose one that's the right challenge for you and head for the summit.

GO WITH THE FLOW. Sometimes the hardest thing to do is to just let go of plans or ideas you spent a lot of time on. Life on the road gets immeasurably easier when you realize that you cannot always be in control. Small obstacles can derail your itinerary, but if you relax and pivot, you may find that the universe has more interesting plans in mind than any you can arrange.

Clockwise from top left: London, England; Banff National Park, Canada; Ko Muk, Thailand; Kyoto, Japan

Asking just one question can lead to a richer story.

I t was a two-hour ride—and a world away—from Havana to the lush region of Pinar del Río, where small plantations grow the bulk of Cuba's world-renowned tobacco. At a family-run farm, we met our guide, Nelson. He led us first to a wooden barn where rows of tobacco leaves were hung to dry, then into another large room where a number of men sat rolling the country's iconic export. I asked about a raised lectern in the far corner, thinking it was a watchful supervisor's post, but was told it was for the "lector," a person paid to read and help the rollers pass the monotonous hours of repetitive work. When the farm had fallen on hard times and could no longer afford a professional lector, a local woman named Doña Josefina had volunteered. For many years she would come, armed with books carefully chosen from the town library—from works by Victor Hugo and Shakespeare to Cervantes's *Don Quixote*. When I asked Nelson how he knew so much about her, he answered: "She was my mother. Toward the end, she could no longer see very well, but she would still come and recite stories she knew by heart."

Left: Hand-rolling cigars, Pinar del Río, Cuba
Right: Havana, Cuba

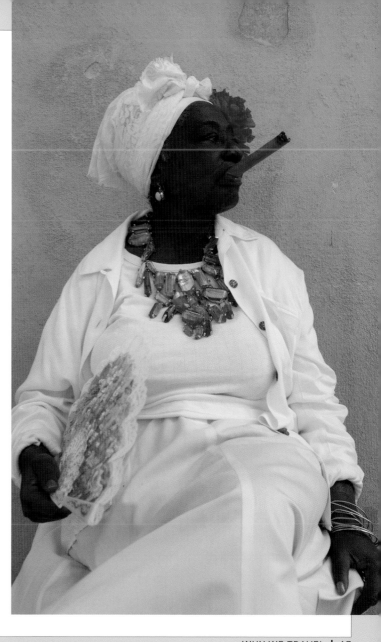

Humpback whale, Norway

Not all classrooms have four walls.

Try on a different way of life.

ONE OF THE BEAUTIES OF TRAVEL is that you can slip on different lifestyles to see how they feel and if they fit. Unusual accommodations allow you to step into alternate worlds, serving up a dose of time travel and a special sense of place.

TEMPLE AND SHRINE STAYS •
Nagano, Japan *(top left)*
Spiritual experiences await those who arrange lodging at a handful of temples and shrines (*shukubo*), some of them centuries old. Guests follow the simple ways of life of Buddhist monks and Shinto priests, waking before sunrise for meditation, eating traditional foods, sleeping in spartan quarters, and strolling through timelessly serene gardens.

TO THE CASTLE BORN •
Ireland and the UK
(middle left)
Baronial castles replete with moats and dungeons (now serving as wine cellars) and surrounded by wooded parklands have remained in the same families for generations. Today, they welcome you for an afternoon brandy by a blazing fire after you've explored the grounds by horse or bike. A candlelit dinner is the day's highlight, served on museum-quality china emblazoned with the family coat of arms.

A MAHARAJA'S RESIDENCE •
Rajasthan, India (bottom left)

From sumptuous palaces to fortresses where the descendants of the original owners still live in private wings, the historic homes of the royal maharajas warmly welcome guests to spend the night in a world suspended in a time when extravagance and over-the-top opulence were the way of everyday life.

CAVE DWELLINGS •
Matera, Italy (top right)

The southern Italian city of Matera and its stark Sassi (literally "stones") district housed cave dwellers from ancient times all the way into the mid-twentieth century, when the caves were abandoned. Today's creative entrepreneurs have combined and refurbished these limestone grottoes into boutique hotels, shops, eateries, and art galleries. From basic to chic, these caves, with their minimalist designs, make it easy

to imagine how life might have been thousands of years ago.

GER CAMPS • Mongolia
(middle right)

Bed down in a traditional *ger* (a Mongolian yurt) and learn how nomadic families dismantle these tentlike homes at the end of the season to follow their migrating herds. All the while, soak up the steppes' hospitality and hear a tale or three about Genghis Khan, whose spirit lives on in the "Land of the Big Sky."

A LIGHTHOUSE KEEPER'S
POST • Northwest and
Northeast Coasts, USA
(bottom right)

Overnight guests will relish the solitude of a lighthouse, where a dramatic coastal setting and spotty Wi-Fi help nurture a deep appreciation for the sea and maritime history. Spot migrating whales from your lookout or watch a storm roll in while savoring the isolation.

Expect nothing, embrace everything.

Left: The Golden Rock, Mount Kyaiktiyo, Myanmar
Right: Hohe Tauern National Park, Austria

Patience is not the ability to wait,
but the ability to keep
a good attitude while waiting.

—JOYCE MEYER

Left: Carpet shop, Essaouira, Morocco
Above: Traditional tea, Istanbul, Turkey

There are no shortcuts
to any place worth going.

—BEVERLY SILLS

Valley of Fire State Park, Nevada, USA

ZAMBIA

Music is a universal language.

I was in Zambia on safari—a word that means "journey" in Swahili—with great hopes of seeing the "Big Five" (lion, leopard, rhinoceros, elephant, and African buffalo). But it was an impromptu visit to a village school that became my most vivid memory. A simple classroom filled with beaming kindergartners—many of whom walked miles every morning to be there—proudly recited their ABCs to our group's delight. But when the teacher asked us to sing a song for the kids that was well-known in our country, we froze. After an awkward silence, I stepped up to the

Left: Schoolchildren, Zambia
Right: Lusaka, Zambia

blackboard, grabbed a piece of chalk, and began to sing, "*A* you're adorable, *B* you're so beautiful, *C* you're a cutie full of charms . . ." while writing the letters on the board. Music and song are always guaranteed icebreakers, no matter the culture or age, and that classroom full of surprised five-year-olds had as much fun as we did, laughing and finding common ground, led by someone not afraid to sing off-key.

My favorite thing is to go
where I've never been.

—DIANE ARBUS

Cherry blossom season, Tokyo, Japan

Stand in awe of genius.

THESE ASTONISHING WORKS are testaments to human ingenuity and artistry, true treasures that hold us in thrall and still possess the power to stop us in our tracks today.

GREAT PYRAMID OF GIZA
Egypt (upper left)
The oldest of the Seven Wonders of the Ancient World and the only one still standing, it is the largest of a three-pyramid complex found just outside of Cairo. Its engineering perfection still boggles the mind more than four thousand years after it was built as a tomb for a pharaoh.

TAJ MAHAL
India (middle left)
This exquisite, ivory-white marble mausoleum was built by the seventeenth-century Mughal emperor Shāh Jāhan in honor of his favorite wife, who had died in childbirth. It is universally admired as a timeless symbol of eternal love and arguably the world's most beautiful building.

UNDERGROUND CHURCHES OF LALIBELA
Ethiopia (lower left)
To create a "New Jerusalem," thirteenth-century Christian king Lalibela ordered eleven churches to be hewn from the bedrock extending as far as 165 feet underground. So extraordinary was this rock-cut architecture that one theory said

a legion of angels completed the work in just one night.

PETRA
Jordan

Poet John Burgon called it the "rose-red city half as old as Time," and Petra has always been known for its elaborate facades carved directly into soft, pink sandstone rock face. A bustling caravan outpost whose heyday began in the first century BCE and lasted some four hundred years, Petra was such a busy and important trade center that it was mentioned in the Old Testament.

HAGIA SOPHIA
Istanbul, Turkey (upper right)

Nearly fifteen centuries old, the epitome of Byzantine architecture, and an engineering marvel, Hagia Sophia was built as the Christian cathedral of Constantinople by Byzantine emperor Justinian I. It was later converted to a mosque, and then declared a museum. In 2020, it was returned to use as a mosque.

NAZCA LINES
Peru (middle right)

More than three hundred geoglyphs and animal representations—including a hummingbird, spider, and condor—and twice as many straight lines were "drawn" across a 190-square-mile arid plain approximately two thousand years ago. They are so massive, they're best viewed by air. Who built them and why? It's one of the world's great archaeological mysteries.

DAVID BY MICHELANGELO
Florence, Italy (lower right)

Michelangelo was just twenty-six years old when he sculpted *David* from an imperfect column of abandoned marble. The seventeen-foot-tall, twelve-thousand-pound masterpiece of Renaissance art is considered by many to be the world's most recognized sculpture.

If you consider
a smile
international
currency,
you'll return
home wealthy.

Street market, Mae Sot, Thailand

See things from a different angle.

CHANGING OUR PERSPECTIVE can open our minds and deepen our appreciation. Sometimes all it takes is gaining some elevation or diving deep. Consider these unconventional vantage points.

A BIRD'S-EYE VIEW: Sail by hot-air balloon over the ancient pagodas and stupas scattered across the plains of Bagan, Myanmar, or be a passenger on one of the hundreds of balloons that fill the sky over Albuquerque, New Mexico, during the annual balloon festival in October.

TREETOP CANOPIES: Suspended high above the forest floor, wooden walkways and suspension bridges promise a unique chance to get eye level with monkeys and birdlife. At a rain forest lodge in Malaysian Borneo's 130-million-year-old jungle, you may even spot an orangutan.

UNDERWATER WORLD: Australia's Great Barrier Reef is an unrivaled place to begin to experience the ocean's power and infinite mystery. It's a submerged habitat totally foreign to our own, teeming with curious creatures you can meet face-to-face.

GO UNDERGROUND: In New Zealand's Waitomo Glowworm Caves, boats pass beneath ceilings that look like twinkling galaxies thanks to the glowworms' bioluminescence; while in Slovenia, the Škocjan Caves make up a colossal subterranean world known as the "Underground Grand Canyon"—complete with a river running through it.

HIGH ALTITUDE: In the Andes Mountains of South America, ethereal light and an alien landscape are the draws at Bolivia's Uyuni Salt Flat, the largest in the world. And the 360-degree majesty of the Himalayan peaks surrounding Tibet's sacred city of Lhasa—former home of the Dalai Lama—are just as breathtaking.

Clockwise from left: Hot-air balloons over Bagan, Myanmar; baby orangutan, Borneo, Malaysia; Great Barrier Reef, Coral Sea; Glowworm Cathedral, Waitomo Cave, New Zealand; salt flats at sunrise, Bolivia.

ANTARCTICA

Some places you really do have to see to believe.

Books and films have always been a ticket to faraway lands, transporting us to other worlds from the comfort of our armchairs. But sleek cinematography and vividly written accounts are a pale facsimile of the real (and surreal) deal of the White Continent. Antarctica's vast landscape of ice, sea, and sky comes in a million shades of blue, its end-of-the-world beauty bathed in the midnight sun. Kitted out in layers of cold-weather gear, we paddled off in kayaks to marvel at towering icebergs the size of ten-story buildings and scooped up small "bergy bits" to bring back to the ship for the night's gin and tonics. We saw pods of humpback whales and visited remote penguin colonies whose comical residents outnumbered us tens of thousands to one. If we stood very still, they waddled up to us to see who these two-legged visitors in bright yellow parkas were—and then, unimpressed, went on their way. Being in Antarctica feels like you have been dropped off on a distant planet—and home feels so very far away.

Antarctica

Paris is always a
good idea.

—Spoken by Julia Ormond in
the 1995 film *Sabrina*

Left: Louvre Museum, Paris, France
Right: Tuileries Garden, Paris, France

Don't forget to turn around and enjoy the view.

I t was late afternoon when our great American road trip through Monument Valley Navajo Tribal Park, on the border of Arizona and Utah, came to an abrupt halt. We felt a sudden thump, followed by the dreaded flapping noise: We had a flat. My friend and I had zero experience changing a tire, there was no sign of civilization on the empty stretch of road, and a cell signal was not to be found. We were quickly losing the day's light and were only half kidding about sleeping under the stars when our saviors pulled up in a rusty Chevy. In no time at all, the bunch of loud, cheerful teenage boys had the spare tire out and the job done as we all joked about our good fortune, and they chatted about trading in life on the reservation for jobs in my hometown of New York City. They were about to take off when one pointed behind us and we turned. The most breathtaking sunset was painting the sky all shades of pink, orange, and crimson, illuminating the timeless buttes and rock formations of the Wild West I had grown up seeing in films. We'd been so consumed with our tire drama that we hadn't noticed it at all. The boys told us their ancestors called it the "Land of Long Shadows," and they sped off, leaving us to drink it all in.

Monument Valley Navajo Tribal Park, Arizona and Utah, USA

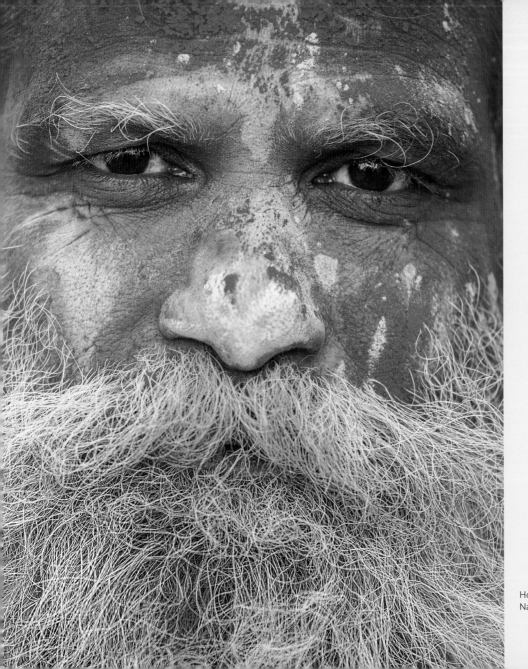

Holi (the Festival of Colors),
Nandgaon, Uttar Pradesh, India

Kindness is the
one true internationally
understood language.
It doesn't take much to
be fluent.

Home is behind, the world ahead,
And there are many paths to tread
Through shadows to the edge of night,
Until the stars are all alight.

—J.R.R. TOLKIEN

Milky Way, Hawaii, USA

Serendipity is the best tour guide.

Left: Bread at market, Rabat, Morocco
Above: Spices for sale at market, Marrakesh, Morocco

My friend and I arrived at the airport in Casablanca, Morocco, for an early afternoon flight to Fez, only to find out it had been canceled and our discount tickets meant a twenty-four-hour wait. Once we went outside to discuss our options, which appeared quite limited, we fell into the extreme good care of Mohammed, a gentle man wearing an impeccable white *djellaba* and yellow leather slippers that turned up at the ends. He assured us his dilapidated Mercedes taxi would get us to Fez in four hours.

But first—we were starving: Could he please bring us to the best place in Casablanca for couscous? After a very animated call on his cell phone, Mohammed drove for over an hour before pulling up in front of a modest home where his mother, wife, two young daughters, extended family, and much of the surrounding neighborhood were all waiting for us, smiling from ear to ear. By chance we had arrived in time for the traditional Friday meal, and the couscous—a meal associated with the country's renowned hospitality—had been cooking for hours. We sat around a large communal platter piled high and topped with fresh vegetables and helpings of chicken and beef; two spoons discreetly appeared for us, their foreign guests. Mohammed's mother still sends me a Christmas card every year. And yes, her couscous was the best I ever tasted.

There's more than one way to get where you're going.

FACING PAGE, left to right. Top: Marrakesh, Morocco. Arc de Triomphe, Paris, France. Metro Station, Madrid, Spain. **Middle:** Cable car, San Francisco, California, USA. Shuttle boat, Bangkok, Thailand. Nanpu Bridge, Shanghai, China. **Bottom:** Conductor at train station, Tokyo, Japan. Amalfi Coast, Italy. Rickshaw driver, New Delhi, India.

THIS PAGE, top to bottom: Ostuni, Italy. Museum of Pop Culture, Seattle, Washington, USA. Bica Funicular, Lisbon, Portugal.

There's always room in your suitcase for curiosity and respect.

Left: Orthodox Tewahedo priest, Dek Island, Lake Tana, Ethiopia
Right: Gelada monkey, also known as Bleeding Heart monkey, Simien Mountains National Park, Ethiopia

Some things are just better experienced alone.

Dead Sea, Israel

KENYA

Face your fears.

A fear of flying is far from an asset for a travel writer, but for years I felt anxious in the air. That changed when I least expected it. When on safari in Kenya, I boarded a toy-sized Cessna with a pilot who looked too young to shave, and we took off on a dirt runway in the direction of our Maasai Mara bush camp. Recognizing that familiar wave of nerves as we set off into the early morning's golden light—with a herd of zebras scattering below us—it came to me: Flying is like magic. Magic requires simply that you believe it's real. You don't have to understand aerodynamics or what holds an aircraft aloft—in fact, it's probably better if you don't. Those butterflies in my stomach were no longer fear, but the sheer thrill of it all. It was a kind of epiphany, and I may have even shed a tear of joy and relief.

Lake Natron at the border of Kenya and Tanzania

Wherever you go,
go with all your heart.

—CONFUCIUS

La Catedral tango club,
Buenos Aires, Argentina

Take a walk.

IN A FAST-PACED WORLD, walking offers the beauty and contemplation of slow travel and can be therapy for our heads and balm to our spirits. It lets us shed our mental and emotional clutter and frees us to be in the present—where our thoughts can begin to flow.

Here are six long-distance treks, both religious and secular, that will get you outside and let you go within.

EL CAMINO DE SANTIAGO
Spain (top left)
The one-thousand-year-old pilgrimage to the cathedral of Santiago de Compostela, where the relics of St. James are said to be kept, wends its way through the ever-changing countryside of northern Spain.

HADRIAN'S WALL PATH
England (middle left)
In 122 CE, the Roman emperor Hadrian ordered a wall to be built from sea to sea across northern England, marking the empire's northernmost

frontier. The 73-mile-long wall can be followed by a footpath that affords captivating views of farmland and moorlands.

SHIKOKU PILGRIMAGE
Japan (bottom left)

Just doing a small part of the 750-mile trail linking eighty-eight Buddhist temples along the picturesque coast of Shikoku—the smallest of Japan's four main islands—will give you a window into the country's history and disappearing traditions of rural life.

CLASSIC INCA TRAIL
Peru (top right)

This three-to-four-day trek along ancient footpaths through the mountain scenery and high-altitude cloud forests of the Andes ends at Machu Picchu, the fifteenth-century ruins of the mysterious "Lost City of the Incas."

MOUNT KAILASH
Tibet (middle right)

The high-altitude Himalayan scenery will leave you slightly breathless as you join pilgrims from all over on the 32-mile circumambulation around this mountain that is sacred to many. (Hindus believe Shiva lives here.)

APPALACHIAN TRAIL
USA (bottom right)

Enjoy the rich plant and animal life and diverse topography of this 2,190-mile trail—done in segments by most hikers—that runs through fourteen states, from Georgia in the south to Maine in the north.

If you truly love nature,
you will find beauty
everywhere.

—VINCENT VAN GOGH

Acadia National Park, Maine, USA

First we eat,
then we do
everything else.

—M.F.K. FISHER

Left: Siena, Italy
Right: Florence, Italy

VIETNAM

Karma is real.

The kind gentleman sitting next to me in the boarding area for a flight from New York City to Los Angeles admitted he was feeling apprehensive—he had not flown in over forty years. I confided I'd be flying even farther: After spending a forty-eight-hour layover in Los Angeles, I'd be continuing on to Vietnam. He pointed to his Navy baseball cap and began to tell me about his two tours of duty in that country. Shortly after, I heard an announcement asking me to come to the departures desk; my frequent flying had paid off with a last-minute upgrade to first class. I asked the gate agent, Patricia (we shared the same name), to transfer the upgrade to my new friend, as a thank-you for his service, and she happily obliged. He was surprised and emotional and explained he had a new grandson waiting for him in California. I was back at the Los Angeles airport two days later, anxious to board my flight to Ho Chi Minh City, when another announcement asked me to see the gate agent. I was upgraded again. "But this time you can't give it away," the agent said with a wink, and handed me a note. "Kindness begets kindness," it read. "Have a great flight, the Other Patricia at JFK."

Hue, Vietnam

Travel's biggest gift to us is making us realize we are all more alike than we are different.

Left: Blowing the shofar, Jerusalem, Israel
Right: Rastafarian Sabbath observance, Saint Andrew Parish, Jamaica

Friends multiply delight.

That age-old adage—choose your travel companions well—was made clear when two friends and I were just minutes into a one-week rental of a self-drive boat on the historic Midi Canal in the South of France. Full of high hopes but woefully inexperienced, we soon discovered that the boat—much larger than we'd expected—seemed to have a mind of its own. Every day was a comedy of mishaps. One time it was getting stuck overnight inside a set of double electric locks that (who knew?) closed promptly at 7:00 p.m. Locks allow water to rise and fall in certain areas to keep boats afloat over terrain of different levels, and we would eventually pass through thirty of them. Another day was full of swerving and hitting the canal banks and other boats, which thankfully caused only negligible damage due to our boat's rubber bumpers. Had it not been for our indomitable spirits, can-do resourcefulness, and, most of all, sense of humor, our decades-long friendship would have been in tatters by the time we arrived at Carcassonne, our final stop, some forty miles from our starting point—and just when we were starting to get the hang of things. Every dinner on deck was a comical replay of the day's mini-dramas, accompanied by local wines and glorious sunsets. To this day, our Midi adventure never fails to make me laugh.

Canal du Midi, France

Share your wonder.

Left: Camel thorn trees and dunes, Sossusvlei, Namibia
Right: A Hausa man in traditional dress, Kano, Nigeria

Fill your heart with gratitude
for what you've done,
not regret for what you haven't.

Above: Plaça Reial, Barcelona, Spain **Right:** Vatican Museum, Rome, Italy

The best things can't always be booked or paid for.

The legendary northern lights are on many people's bucket lists, but there's never a guarantee that you'll actually see them. My husband, Nick, and I traveled by a four-passenger plane from Fairbanks to Bettles, a bush town in Alaska's Arctic Circle (population sixty-three at the time), where we had booked a special two-night aurora package. Days were spent poking around an old gold rush ghost town—and waiting for night to come. Despite staying up well past 2:00 a.m. each night, we didn't see the lights. We returned to Fairbanks crestfallen, recounting our disappointment to our friend and host, who admitted he had seen the lights so often he barely looked up anymore. Late that night, pounding on our bedroom door, our friend roused us from our warm beds and rushed us outside into the frigid night. Even now, it seems impossible that such a spectacle really exists—changing shapes and colors that appear like diaphanous green curtains undulating across the liquid black sky. We stood there for more than an hour, transfixed, oblivious to the cold but not to the wonder of it all.

Aurora borealis, Alaska, USA

Listen to your intuition.

was standing on the dock of my dreamy Maldives Island resort, waiting for a prepaid launch to a private atoll that had been described as Indian Ocean heaven. But I had already enjoyed two days in beach paradise and was drawn to the laughter coming from the staff's shuttle boat about to leave for the country's capital, Male. I recognized Mushan, the resort's barman, and asked him if there was room. Forty minutes later I was arriving in the compact but chaotic city and getting an introduction to the dockside fish market (think tunas the size of small torpedoes) by Peter, the resort chef. He seemed to know every fish vendor by name, and soon one was arranging for his taxi-driving son to play tour guide and take me around the small island. Our first stop was his mosque, the seventeenth-century Hukuru Miskiy—built entirely from coral—which he proudly described as the archipelago nation's gem. The rest of the day provided one memorable surprise after another, and I thanked my instincts back at the resort that encouraged me to pivot, change course, and see what surprises the fates would bring.

Left: Maldives **Right:** Fish market, Male, Maldives
Below: Screw pine fruit at Maldives market

People travel from the other side of the world to see what we have under our noses.

Canyonlands National Park, Utah, USA

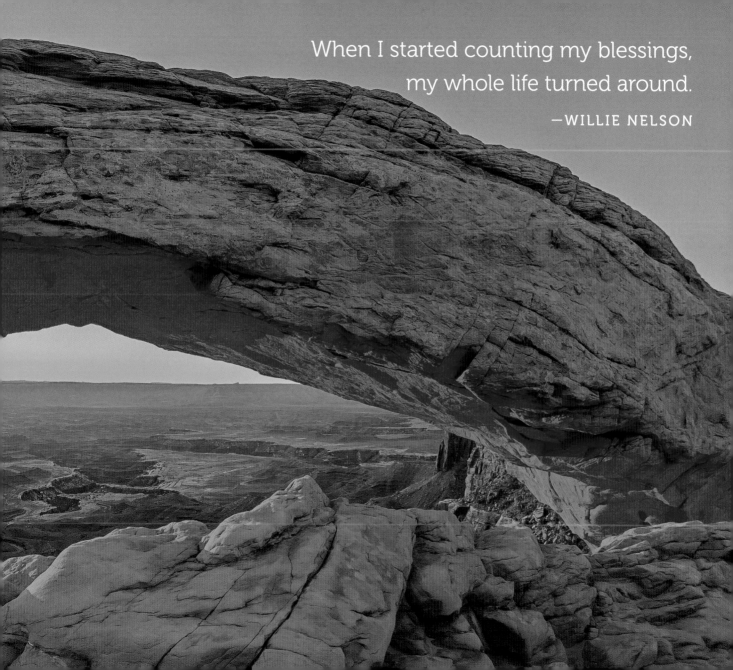

When I started counting my blessings,
my whole life turned around.

—WILLIE NELSON

Be swept away without leaving your couch.

FASTEN YOUR SEAT BELT and let these evocative films transport you to another world where the settings are as vivid as the characters. They may remind you of adventures past or inspire you to make plans for tomorrow. **(Clockwise from top:)**

TO CATCH A THIEF
1955 • French Riviera

This gem of a Hitchcock thriller stars debonair Cary Grant and an exquisite Grace Kelly against the glamorous backdrop of the French Riviera in the '50s. Visit Cannes with its yacht-filled Vieux Port, Art Deco hotels that line the La Croisette beachfront promenade, and a lifestyle of understated wealth as polished and timelessly chic as the film's leading stars.

AROUND THE WORLD IN 80 DAYS
1956

This film—ambitiously shot in 112 locations in thirteen countries, including London, Paris, Japan, Thailand, and Spain—affords a whirlwind world tour. Victorian gentleman Phileas Fogg (David Niven) and his devoted valet, Passepartout (Cantinflas), have made a bet they can circumnavigate the globe in record time, and they bring us along on their amazing race.

BREAKFAST AT TIFFANY'S
1961 • New York City

Audrey Hepburn's turn as the eccentric yet naïve party girl Holly Golightly continues to resonate. Many of the film's iconic scenes—Holly window-shopping at Tiffany's in her pearl choker or wistfully singing "Moon River" on her apartment fire escape—are cinematic gold. City landmarks like Central Park's Bandshell, the imposing New York Public Library, and skyscrapers that line elegant Park Avenue are a paean to the city that stole her heart.

OUT OF AFRICA
1985 • Kenya

Based on the life and writings of Karen Blixen, this film and its breathtaking cinematography are an inspiring display of Kenya's beauty. It recounts the 1920s love story between a married, wealthy Danish woman (Meryl Streep) and a handsome, freedom-loving pilot (Robert Redford). Their frequent joy rides in a dilapidated biplane offer sweeping views of the Chyulu Hills (filling in for the Ngong Hills) and the Great Rift Valley beyond, as well as the Maasai Mara, with wildebeests scattering below.

THE LAST EMPEROR
1987 • Forbidden City, Beijing, China

This lush, epic production—the first feature ever filmed in Beijing's Forbidden City—brings us into the world of Puyi, the last emperor of the Qing dynasty in China, played by Richard Vuu as a boy and John Lone as an adult. The movie showcases amazing views of the palace—inside and out. Director Bernardo Bertolucci's team designed a studio-set re-creation of the palace's lacquered and ceremonious interiors for extended shoots and reshoots, but you wouldn't know that you're not firmly in the palace with every shot.

A ROOM WITH A VIEW
1985 • Tuscany

Set in the Renaissance capital of Florence, this award winner follows young Lucy Honeychurch (Helena Bonham Carter) and her chaperone (Maggie Smith) as eager Edwardian-era tourists visiting the city's fresco-covered churches, palazzo-rimmed piazzas, and museums brimming with sculptures and masterworks. Timeless views of the Arno River and the Ponte Vecchio and the nearby hills of Fiesole help feed a love affair with Italy.

LOST IN TRANSLATION
2003 • Tokyo

Bob (Bill Murray), a fading American movie star visiting Tokyo to promote a local whiskey, meets Charlotte (Scarlett Johansson), a young American staying at the same ultra-modern high-rise hotel, and friendship ensues. Capturing the twenty-four-seven energy of Tokyo, the film unfolds as they sample karaoke and sushi in the bright, neon-lit Shinjuku and Shibuya business and entertainment districts.

Step into someone else's shoes;
you'll be forever changed
when you give them back.

Left: Berber man leading a camel train, Erg Chebbi, Morocco
Right: Berber man in traditional dress, Morocco

What are you waiting for?
What are you saving for?
Now is all there is.

—GEORGE BALANCHINE'S
exhortation to his dancers

Lake Bachalpsee,
Grindenwald, Switzerland

MONGOLIA

First impressions are often wrong.

The moment I boarded my long-haul flight from Tokyo back to New York City and sat down in my window seat, the woman to my left started chatting. No matter that I buried my head in a book; she persisted. But as the hours in the air ticked by, the woman who had started out as an irritation morphed into a witty, well-traveled storyteller. Her anecdotes were funny, and her tips were valuable and had me reaching for my notebook. Her enthralling tale of riding across the steppes of Mongolia with a nomadic family, who she was convinced were descendants of Genghis Khan, was the reason I eventually traveled there. And her favorite hole-in-the-wall souvlaki place in Athens still remains my go-to spot whenever I'm in town.

Left: Arkhangai Province, Mongolia **Right:** Eagle hunters, Mongolia

A journey can make
your own home
all the sweeter.

Left: Handwoven textiles, Cuzco, Peru
Right: Santa Fe, New Mexico, USA

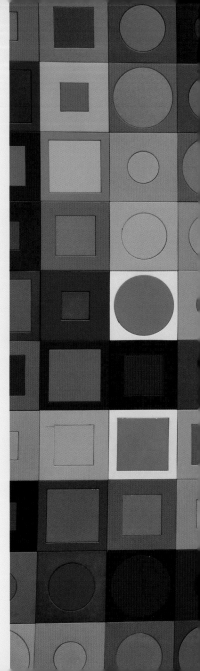

One can travel the world and see nothing.
To achieve understanding it is
necessary not to see many things,
but to look hard at what you do see.

—GIORGIO MORANDI

Silver linings can be golden.

I haven't always been tolerant of the monkey wrenches that life has tossed into my well-planned travel itineraries. But I've learned that obstacles can lead to invaluable experiences. Such was the case on the winter day when Venice was socked in with heavy fog, closing the airport and forcing upon me an overnight stay. I was no stranger to the charms of the "Adriatic Queen," but here was the gift of unscheduled time to explore the labyrinth of quiet back alleyways cloaked in mist. As I roamed, I could hear the muted sounds of *gondolieri* calling out to one another. I followed the sounds to the back door of the Squero di San Trovaso, the oldest of the city's few remaining boatyards where gondolas are made and repaired. The door was ajar, and I stepped inside. Amid the smell of freshly lacquered wood and the banter of the workers in Venetian dialect that few outside the city can understand, I stood and watched the creation of a new gondola, one of just a few still made there. The sun came out the next day, and I left Venice so grateful to have witnessed a disappearing corner of the "City Built on Water."

Left: St. Mark's Square, Venice, Italy **Right:** Venice, Italy

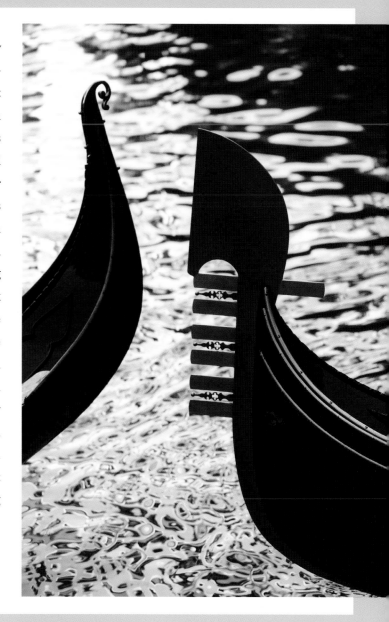

Sometimes the best traveling companion is you.

FOR MANY OF US, the idea of traveling alone is daunting. Not having someone to eat with and help with decisions may seem scary. But the benefits of solo travel are invaluable, and they are many. Here are just a few.

It's empowering to be pushed out of your comfort zone; when you discover you can handle whatever comes your way, you grow more confident and self-reliant.

It's easier to meet the locals as well as fellow travelers as a single person—and easier to ask for and receive help.

With more time for introspection, you'll discover yourself as you discover the world.

Mayotte, a French region in the Mozambique Channel, Indian Ocean

It gives you ultimate freedom: There are no compromises, spontaneity is a given, and you call the shots.

It's less stressful when you don't have to put up with someone else's annoying habits.

Without distractions, you can be in the moment and more aware of your surroundings.

There's plenty of catch-up time to indulge in books, movies, sketching, writing in your journal, creating those blogs—and room service!

Perhaps travel cannot
prevent bigotry,
but by demonstrating that
all peoples cry, laugh, eat,
worry, and die, it can
introduce the idea that if
we try to understand each
other, we may even
become friends.

—MAYA ANGELOU

Left: Golden Bridge, Da Nang, Vietnam
Right: Taj Mahal, Agra, India

When you think you have exhausted all possibilities, think again.

My stay in Bangkok was chaotic and fun—there's no better city for shopping, temples, food, and night markets. But my luck was up when it was time to leave. With little wiggle room to catch my flight, I was stuck at the hotel while unexpectedly early monsoon rains pelted the city. The futuristic Skytrain was still under construction, and there were few ways to get to the airport. The hotel's front desk managers were busy checking out all possibilities, but to no avail: The river ferry schedule was too tight, taxi services were booked solid, and the bus transfer would never make it on time. I was nervous and stressed—I was about to lose my nonrefundable international air ticket. One of the hotel's bellboys stood by, looking concerned and ready to help. So I asked if he had a motorbike and an extra rain poncho. He brightened up immediately, and we were soon zipping off to the airport, weaving through the city's snail-paced traffic and squinting against the rain. We made it to the departures terminal on time—just! We were soaked but grinning proudly. He earned a handful of Thai baht and my gratitude for life. And I scored a great story—and made my flight. Where there's a will . . .

Tuk Tuk traveling through streets of Bangkok, Thailand

For my part,
I travel not to go
anywhere, but to go.
I travel for travel's sake.
The great affair is
to move.

—ROBERT LOUIS STEVENSON

Left: Belfast, Northern Ireland
Right: Book stall, Havana, Cuba

It's better to travel than to arrive.

I had never attempted a long-distance, multiday hike before, but the thought of escaping the demands of my day-to-day world and having time to reflect and connect with nature appealed to me. After months of training to be ready for what lay ahead, I set off on El Camino de Santiago (Way of St. James), the thousand-year-old pilgrimage trail that traces its way over the Pyrenees mountains in France to northwestern Spain.

Not having the five weeks needed to complete the full five-hundred-mile route, I started out one hundred miles from the final destination of the city of Santiago de Compostela. Each day was spent walking through rich farmland, undulating vineyards, and medieval towns and across ancient stone bridges,

Left: El Camino de Santiago, Spain **Above left:** A Camino "passport"
Above right: Last milestone marker, El Camino de Santiago, Spain

often with modern-day pilgrims who had come from all corners of the globe. There was a Dutch mother and her twelve-year-old son; a Moroccan professor from Rabat; a priest from Lourdes, returning for his eighth Camino. We exchanged recommendations for inns, remedies for sore feet, and the stories behind our decisions to follow this sacred trail. I welcomed the company but also each opportunity to walk alone, grateful for the chance to pause and think about what matters most—and least. I felt both elated and a little sad as we approached the final stretch. The Camino was the journey I didn't know I needed, where a map and a destination were all that I required—in a corner of the world where not much has changed in one thousand years.

Kumari Festival, Kathmandu, Nepal

Courtesy is contagious.

PUT THOSE VOICE-TRANSLATION APPS ASIDE: Learning just a few words in the language of your host country goes a long way toward creating goodwill. Start with the magic word—"please"—and its equally powerful sibling, "thank you."

Chinese (Mandarin)
Please: Qǐng (sheeng)
Thank you: Xie xie (seeyah seeyah)

French
Please: S'il vous plaît (see voo PLAY)
Thank you: Merci (mer SEE)

German
Please: Bitte (BIT teh)
Thank you: Danke (DAHNK eh)

Greek
Please: Parakaló (para KA lo)
Thank you: Efharisto (ef HAR isto)

Italian
Please: Per favore (per fa VOR ay)
Thank you: Grazie (GRAHT see eh)

Japanese
Please: Onegai shimasu (o neh GUY shee mahs)
Thank you: Arigato (ah REE gah toe)

Polish
Please: Proszę (prosh-eh)
Thank you: Dziękuję (jenkoo-yeh)

Russian
Please: Pozhaluysta (po zha LU stah)
Thank you: Spasibo (spa SEE bah)

Spanish
Please: Por favor (por fah VOR)
Thank you: Gracias (grah see ahss)

Swahili
Please: Tafadhali (taf ah DAHL ee)
Thank you: Asante (ah SAN tay)

Swedish
Please: Takk (tahk)
Thank you: Takk (tahk—yes, it is the same!)

Indonesian children playing in the rain

Luxury comes in all shapes and sizes.

There is no wrong way to be a foodie.

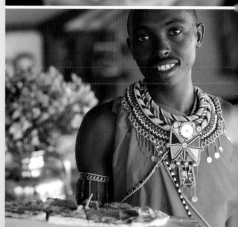

FACING PAGE, top row: Feta cheese and olives, Greece. Smoked herring, France. Glacé pears, France.
Middle row: Donghuamen, Bejing, China. Bread, Muslim quarter, Xi'an, China. Market, La Rochelle, France.
Bottom row: New Orleans, Louisiana, USA. Salicornia—or sea beans, France. Café, Lisbon, Portugal.

THIS PAGE, top to bottom: Burgundy snails, France. Churros, Spain. Chapati, Kenya.

Left: Museum of Pop Culture, Seattle, Washington, USA
Right: Ice bar at the Sorrisniva Igloo Hotel, Alta, Norway

I have found out that there ain't no surer way
to find out whether you like people or
hate them, than to travel with them.

—MARK TWAIN

Travel makes the ordinary extraordinary.

I was fifteen when I took my first flight—alone—to Santo Domingo in the Dominican Republic to stay with a high school friend and her family. She warned me that I might be bored—there wasn't much to do—and it's true that we mostly just hung out around her home. But for me, this world of just-picked mangoes, merengue, and a revolving door of extended family dropping by without notice was novel and fascinating. Breakfast consisted of *mangú* (mashed plantains) served with eggs from the chickens that roamed the backyard; everyone seemed to play guitar (I learned a few traditional ballads whose lyrics I remember to this day); we made frequent trips to the busy *mercado*, where the vendors all came to know this gringa's newfound love of fresh guava and pineapple. The days were long and languid, except for one afternoon, when the family organized an outing to a neighborhood game of baseball, a sport as popular there as it is in the United States. Instead of beer and hot dogs, there were fresh *chinola* (passion fruit) juice and *pastelitos* (a kind of mini empanada), and the fans were boisterous and loud. I often think of that game with great affection—and I don't even like baseball!

Left: Mangoes at fruit stand, Dominican Republic
Right: Playing baseball, Santo Domingo, Dominican Republic

Give it a try, then decide.

ONE OF THE MANY BENEFITS OF TRAVEL is sampling new cuisines. Certain aspects of international food can be surprising—even shocking—and may require a little courage. Some delicacies may be an acquired taste; others are unexpectedly tasty and similar to foods you already know. Before you turn up your nose at any of these exotic offerings, bear in mind that some foods considered traditionally American are also pretty unusual—I'm thinking scrapple and chitterlings!

A few international specialties for adventurous taste buds (clockwise from top right):

FRIED TARANTULA
Cambodia

TOASTED BEETLES
Mexico

FERMENTED SHARK
Iceland

AIRAG
Mongolia
An alcoholic spirit made from fermented horse milk

DEEP-FRIED SCORPIONS ON A STICK
Thailand

ONE-HUNDRED-YEAR-OLD EGGS
China
Chicken, duck, or quail eggs pickled for up to one hundred days—not years!

———

Not Pictured

BOILED TUNA EYEBALLS
Japan

BARBECUED WARTHOG RIBS
South Africa

FRIED COD TONGUES
Canada

BAKED GUINEA PIG
Peru

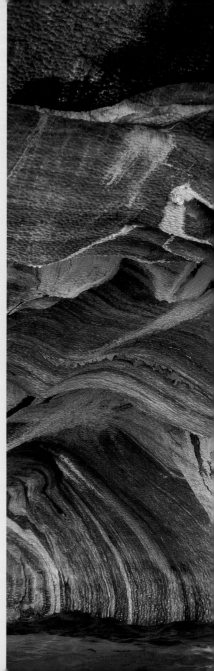

I had always wanted an adventurous life.
It took a long time to realize that I was
the only one who was going to make
an adventurous life happen to me.

—RICHARD BACH

Above: Santa Teresa, Costa Rica
Right: Marble Cathedral, Puerto Rio Tranquilo, Chile

To shut your eyes
is to travel.

—EMILY DICKINSON

Whirling dervishes, Istanbul, Turkey

You never know what's going to work.

My sightseeing schedule in Beijing was packed, but when a sore knee got worse, our young guide put everything aside and insisted she knew the best place for Traditional Chinese Medicine. And, well, when in Rome. . . . A crowd of local customers was jostling to buy fusions of dried herbs when we arrived at the country's oldest pharmacy, established in the seventeenth century. The aromas were a heady mix of enticing and pungent—and all natural. I was whisked upstairs, where an attendant in a white lab coat asked me countless questions interpreted by an assistant. Had I been stressed or depressed? (Um, no, I was on vacation.) What did I know about the health of my kidneys and liver? (Not much.) I must have given my consent to a treatment, because suddenly my leg was being wrapped in gauze, soaked with a mysterious liquid, and set on fire. Something was said about it stimulating the flow of energy. It was extinguished before I had time to protest. My knee felt much better, and I was able to resume the day's itinerary without missing a beat. Seems the treatment—based on more than two thousand years of practice—is still around for a reason.

THIS PAGE, top: Ancient medical chart of acupuncture meridians
Bottom: Traditional Chinese apothecary chest
FACING PAGE: Traditional medicines, China

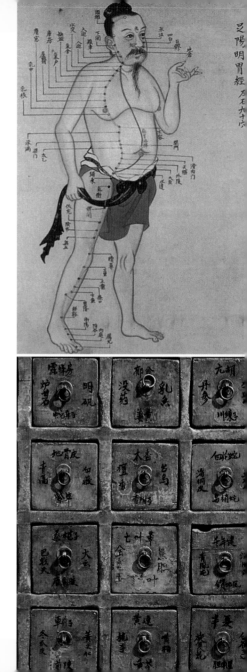

The moment one gives close attention to anything, even a blade of grass, it becomes a mysterious, awesome, indescribably magnificent world in itself.

—HENRY MILLER

Dragonflies

One of the best gifts of travel is the kindred spirits you meet along the way.

Left: Café, Évora, Portugal
Right: Lavender fields, Valensole, France

Mind your manners.

FOREIGNERS ARE GENERALLY GIVEN A LITTLE ROOM for cultural mistakes, but it's always appreciated when you make an effort to learn the local etiquette. Here are just a few customs to be aware of. When in doubt, watch what others are doing and follow their lead.

LEAVE A LITTLE FOOD ON YOUR PLATE. If invited to someone's house for dinner in Middle Eastern and many Asian countries (South Korea, Thailand, Cambodia, China), always leave a little food on your plate. Finishing everything implies that your host did not feed you enough, and they will continue to replenish your dish. But in India and Japan, where waste is frowned upon, finishing your food is polite, and a clean plate is a compliment to the host's talents.

BOW. In East Asia—particularly in Japan, South Korea, China, and Vietnam—bows take the place of handshakes when you meet someone. Always bow first to the oldest person. In Japan, the deeper the bow and the longer it is held, the more respect is shown.

DON'T POINT. Pointing with your index finger is considered impolite in several European, Latin American, and African nations. It is particularly rude in Indonesia, China, and Japan. When gesturing, simply use your entire hand.

THE "OK" SIGN IS NOT ALWAYS OKAY. In France it means "zero" or "worthless," and it is actually offensive in other countries such as Venezuela, Brazil, and Turkey. Similarly, although thumbs-up commonly indicates something well done, it is an insulting gesture in Italy, Greece, and Iran.

Kyoto, Japan

Abroad is the place where we stay up late,
follow impulse and find ourselves
as wide open as when we are in love.

—PICO IYER

Above and right: Santorini, Greece

The world will
never starve for want of wonders;
but only for want of wonder.

—G. K. CHESTERTON

Left: Rot Fai Market, Bangkok, Thailand
Above right: Dragon fruit

Every now and then
a man's mind is stretched
by a new idea or sensation,
and never shrinks back
to its former dimensions.

—OLIVER WENDELL HOLMES SR.

The Winton Gallery in the Science Museum, London, England

Do the difficult things first.

'd thought I could handle being eleven thousand feet above sea level, but my achy head was telling me otherwise. The next day I was to visit legendary Machu Picchu, the "Lost City of the Incas," and I needed to acclimate. Sitting in the lobby of my hotel in Cusco, on my third cup of coca-leaf tea (a traditional treatment for high-altitude symptoms), I met Edith from Atlanta, who, at age ninety, was on her first international trip. She was soon recounting how family hardships as a young girl had forced her to drop out of school early and take the only work she could find, as a washerwoman. Marriage and a growing family had filled her days, then decades, until recently, when, to celebrate her birthday, her five children had chipped in to send her and her husband of seventy years to a place they had always dreamed about. Now here she was, the proud owner of a passport, and Peru was her inaugural stamp. "You've got to do the demanding places first," she confided with a smile. "Your knees have expiration dates."

Left and right: Machu Picchu, Peru

Don't forget to look up . . .

THIS PAGE, clockwise from left: Tilla Kari Madrasa and Mosque, Samarkand, Uzbekistan. Royal Ontario Museum, Toronto, Canada. Tate Britain, London, England. Campeche City, Mexico. **FACING PAGE, clockwise from top:** Supertree Grove, Gardens by the Bay, Singapore. Canoe sculpture, Osaka, Japan. Al Ateneo Grand Splendid Bookshop, Buenos Aires, Argentina. Arches National Park, Utah, USA. *Christ the Redeemer*, Rio de Janeiro, Brazil.

. . . and down.

FACING PAGE, clockwise from top: Great Blue Hole, Lighthouse Reef, Belize. St. James's shell, Santiago de Compostela, Spain. Pamukkale thermal pools, Turkey. *Cumil* sculpture, Bratislava, Slovakia. Mosaic detail, Panagia, Haritomeni Church, Symi, Greece. Sidewalk artist, Florence, Italy.
THIS PAGE, clockwise from right: Stolpersteine ("stumbling stones"), Berlin, Germany. Via Appia, Rome, Italy. John Lennon memorial, Central Park, New York City, USA. Rice terraces, Bali, Indonesia. Tilework, Jameh Mosque, Yazd, Iran.

DUBLIN, IRELAND

Go with the flow.

I checked into my broom-closet-sized hotel room owned by the pub downstairs in central Dublin, bone tired and ready to throw myself into bed. But there would be no rest for the jet-lag weary that night. It turned out that the legendary band U2 was playing a hometown gig at Croke Park the next day, and fans were flying in from all over the world. The cobbled lane beneath my window seemed to have become pre-concert central, packed with excited music lovers fueled by the rivers of Guinness being served by the pub until the wee hours. I gave up trying to sleep, wandered down to join the crowd below, and was swept up in a raucous and quintessentially Irish sing-along of every song in the U2 repertoire. Somehow, I managed to fend off those who insisted I get a tattoo declaring my newfound love for "the greatest rock group on planet earth." Nonetheless, that night was the very embodiment of *craic*—pronounced "crack" and Gaelic slang for "a great time!" It was that—and beyond.

Left and right: Dublin, Ireland

So much of who we are is
where we have been.

—WILLIAM LANGEWIESCHE

Above: Indigenous art, Australia
Right: A Maasai woman dressed
in traditional attire, Kenya

No passport? No problem!

WHEN YOU HAVE THE TRAVEL BUG but don't have the time or money (or perhaps a passport) to go abroad, consider these alternative destinations with similar characteristics right here in the US of A.

If you're dreaming of . . .
CAPPADOCIA, TURKEY, with its fantastical geology, including cone-shaped minarets and "fairy chimneys" that create an otherworldly beauty . . .

try . . .
BRYCE CANYON NATIONAL PARK, UTAH, a forest of totem pole–like formations called "hoodoos"—once believed to be evildoers frozen in time—that take on a crimson hue at sunset, prime viewing time.

If you're dreaming of . . .
GREAT OCEAN ROAD, AUSTRALIA, with its 150 miles of rugged coastline whose highlights include quirky surf towns; wide, empty beaches; and the off-shore sea stacks called the Twelve Apostles . . .

try . . .
HIGHWAY 1, CALIFORNIA, the twisting, all-American road that follows California's dreamy Pacific coast from Dana Point in Orange County all the way to San Francisco; along the ride you'll pass historic Spanish missions, vineyards, and the iconic Big Sur.

If you're dreaming of . . .
ROTORUA, NEW ZEALAND, a geothermal wonderland situated on the Pacific Rim of Fire, active with bubbling mud pools, natural hot springs, and the Pohutu Geyser, which explodes one hundred feet skyward . . .

try . . .
YELLOWSTONE NATIONAL PARK, WYOMING Sitting on top of a volcanic hot spot, the world's first national park boasts star attractions such as Old Faithful Geyser, which erupts about seventeen times a day and is one of almost five hundred geysers in the park.

FACING PAGE, **left to right: Top:** Cappadocia, Turkey. Bryce Canyon National Park, Utah. **Bottom:** Champagne pool, Rotorua, New Zealand. Grand Prismatic Spring, Yellowstone National Park, Wyoming.

No one can explore the world *for* you.

Above: Shrine, Lamego, Portugal **Right:** Poznan, Poland

Failure is the best teacher.

There are some trips so riddled with glitches that the only consolation is that they will eventually make good dinner conversation. One of these began with me confirming my departure for a flight to Hong Kong for the following day at 1:00 p.m., only to find out it was leaving at 1:00 a.m.—in six hours. I made it in time, but because I landed in Hong Kong earlier than expected, my Kowloon hotel room was not ready, so I wandered the neighborhood's network of back alleys and purchased a beautifully made silk top for $28, the kind of bargain not uncommon in the city. It wasn't long before I realized that my jet-lagged brain had flubbed the currency conversion, and that in fact I'd been charged $280—the correct price, but one I could not afford. Try as I might, I couldn't find the hole-in-the-wall shop to return the item. Resigned, I did find some consolation in my favorite Hong Kong street food, tasty rice noodles doused with peanut sauce. But I was soon reminded that not all street food vendors are created equal: The cheung fun was not particularly fresh, and gastro problems put me down for the rest of the day. The good news? All my bad luck was out of the way, and I was able to enjoy the rest of my stay in Hong Kong enormously and returned home (confirming my departure information *way* in advance) wiser for the wear.

Left: Vendor serving noodles, Hong Kong **Right:** Lanterns, Hong Kong

If your eyes are open,
you will see the things worth seeing.

—RUMI

RUSSIA

Fast and easy isn't always the best choice.

Today's high-speed train from St. Petersburg to Moscow takes just four hours. But when my friend Miguel and I made the journey in 1992 following the collapse of the Soviet Union, that same train trip took twelve long but highly memorable hours. Nothing says "Welcome aboard" like armed Russian soldiers patrolling the car, which was lined with crowded compartments where we found ourselves knee to knee with a family on their way home to Irkutsk in eastern Siberia. Naive and poorly prepared, we had brought very little food with us, but language and cultural barriers dissolved when the family shared their basket packed with homemade sausages and cheese, crusty bread, and dried apricots. I risked offending them when

I offered some rubles in return, but they gladly accepted them. And that's when the homemade vodka came out. I don't remember anything after that . . .

Left: Listvyanka, Russia
Right: Breakfast on the Trans-Siberian railroad

A journey is best
measured in friends
rather than miles.

—TIM CAHILL

Novice monks, Bhutan

SIGHIȘOARA, ROMANIA

Get lost—
and find what you're looking for.

My first day in any town is dedicated to one thing: turning off my phone's GPS and heading out on an exploratory stroll. I like to visit bakeries and grocery stores, see where the children go to school, sit in a small park and people watch. I enjoyed a particularly long walk while wandering the well-preserved medieval quarter of Sighișoara, a walled city in Romania's Transylvania region. Just as I was wondering whether I'd ever find my guesthouse again, I turned down a cobblestone lane flanked by pastel-colored homes, where one building stood out for its plaque: "In this house between the years 1431–1435 lived Vlad Dracul." It is no secret that this small city takes a certain pride in being the birthplace of Vlad the Impaler, aka Dracula, the world's most notorious vampire, but it didn't register until I'd read that plaque marking the house where his father had lived and where he— the inspiration for Bram Stoker's Gothic novel—was born in 1431. The distinction between fact and fiction is a blur in Sighișoara, but this eerie brush with Dracula reawakened my childhood fascination with all things ghoulish. In a shop awash in kitschy vampire-inspired tchotchkes, I purchased a mug of the fang-toothed count that now graces my desk at home.

Left: Sighișoara, Romania **Top right:** Bran Castle, Transylvania, Romania
Bottom right: Vlad the Impaler

Practice defensive packing.

SMART PACKING is not only about rolling versus folding or how to beat weight restrictions. Pack peace of mind by taking these simple steps that will mitigate the pain if your handbag or suitcase is lost or stolen.

MARK YOUR SUITCASE with two distinctively colorful name tags (in case one gets ripped or torn off) to ensure it isn't "innocently" mistaken for someone else's. Take a cell phone photo of your bag, so if it goes missing, you can show it to the baggage claim agent.

CREATE A DIGITAL FILE of photos of your passport, visas, credit and debit cards (both sides), driver's license, and anything else you'll lose if your bag or wallet is stolen or lost. Print out three sets—one for your suitcase, one for your handbag or carry-on, and one to leave with someone at home who won't mind if you call them in a panic at 2:00 a.m. when you need help replacing these items.

DIVIDE YOUR CASH. If you're traveling to a less developed or remote destination where cash is still king, split it into three envelopes. Place one well hidden in your checked luggage, one in your carry-on, and the last somewhere on your body, such as in a money belt, a zippered pants pocket, or—as my grandmother taught me—a bra or sock.

Right: Farafra, Egypt

Look closer.
Beauty is often
found in the
in-between
places.

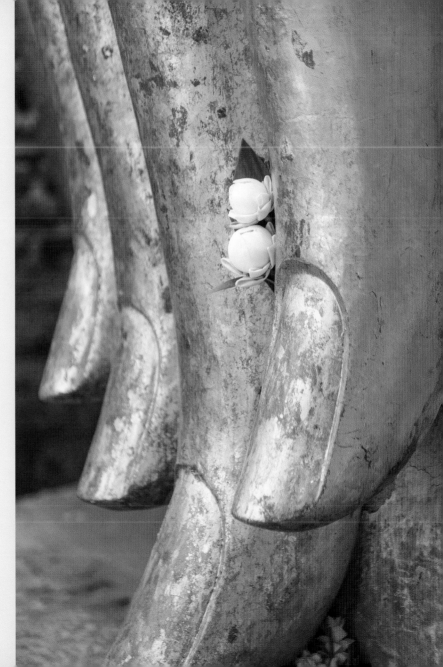

Left: Shop in the Grand Bazaar, Istanbul, Turkey
Right: Hand of Buddha, Wat Si Chum,
Sukhothai province, Thailand

Accept invitations.

A tooth filing is an important Hindu coming-of-age ritual for Balinese adolescents that is almost always paired with a significant celebration. When the owner of my small B and B in Ubud invited me to the day-long *metatah* of his teenage daughter in his hometown an hour's bus ride away, I was honored—but I hesitated. Balinese hospitality was new to me—as an outsider unfamiliar with this traditional Indonesian custom, wouldn't I be intruding? Instead, I was welcomed like a guest of honor. I joined members of the host family, who explained to me what I was seeing, from the behind-the-scenes preparations of the girl's makeup and elaborate hair ornaments (which felt a bit like prom-night preparations) to the blessings by the local priests, all leading up to the filing of the girl's canine teeth—a painless process believed to keep her free from bad luck and bad habits. What followed was a village-wide celebration of warmth and pure joy, with elaborate displays of ceremonial foods meant to impress both the gods and guests (the men of the village had been spit roasting a pig since early morning), flowing gamelan music, and the teenage girl as the center of attention, dancing and laughing with friends and family. It was vaguely reminiscent of important celebrations back home—first Communions and bat mitzvahs—but a whole lot more fascinating and fun.

Left: Tirta Empul water temple, Bali, Indonesia
Right: Woman taking offerings to a temple, Bali, Indonesia
Inset: Lotus flower

Don't let
someone else
be the gatekeeper
of your dreams.

Liguria, Italy

Strike up a conversation.

Top left: Demel pastry shop, Vienna, Austria
Bottom left: Statue of Johann Strauss, Vienna, Austria
Right: Original Sacher-Torte (chocolate cake) at Café Sacher, Vienna, Austria

'm not particularly extroverted at home, but being in a foreign environment emboldens me to connect with people I encounter—and the effort has never let me down. I was in a cozy Viennese coffeehouse where everything in the display case looked irresistible. I asked the teenage girl at the table next to me to please point out on the menu what she had ordered. In near-perfect English, she explained that it was a *melange*, espresso with extra steamed milk topped with froth, and *apfeltorte*, the house specialty made of thin layers of apple encased in a sugary confection. She seemed eager to practice her conversational skills and was soon sharing tips about how to avoid museum lines and where to find the "real Vienna." Learning that I was American, she mentioned that she hoped to visit her uncle in Washington, DC—who, to my amazement, turned out to be a professor of mine from university days. We called him on her cell phone, and I told him that his European history class was the very reason I was visiting Austria. We laughed at this incredible moment of kismet that had brought us all together and planned a reunion at his favorite coffee shop in DC, when the travel gods allowed.

Whoever created the world
went to a lot of trouble.
It would be downright rude
not to go out and see
as much of it as possible.

—EDWARD READICKER-HENDERSON

Dark Hedges Road, County Antrim, Northern Ireland

Jumpstart your senses.

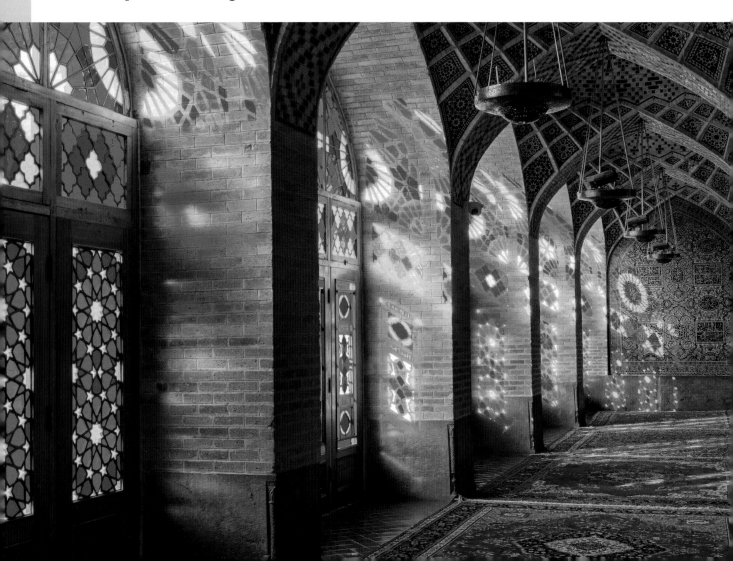

Some destinations are so extraordinary, to visit them feels as though you have stepped into another realm. Iran is one such place. Despite ample pre-departure research, everything caught me by surprise and heightened my senses. It was a veritable feast for the eyes: The dazzling architecture spoke to its rich history and ancient civilizations. Mosques with turquoise-tiled domes and delicate minarets stood alongside ancient palaces that rimmed large city squares, their splashing fountains and fragrant gardens popular with school groups and local families who picnicked there until late into the evening. At the thirteenth-century bazaar in Tabriz, mustached merchants sold spices and other goods redolent of Silk Road caravans—saffron, pomegranate molasses, tamarind, pistachios. A muffled call to prayer went mostly unheeded by vendors, who unfurled intricately woven carpets while artists displayed their miniature Persian paintings. This was culture shock in the most thrilling sense, making me feel alert and alive in what is possibly the friendliest country on earth.

Left: Nasir al-Molk Mosque, Shiraz, Iran **Right:** Mahomet roses

The years are flying past and
we all waste so much time wondering
if we dare to do this or that.
The thing is to leap, to try, to take a chance.

—LEONARD COHEN

Marsala Cathedral, Sicily, Italy

Immerse yourself in nature.

THERE ARE COUNTLESS WAYS to connect to the wilderness. Here are a few of the most magnificent.

AVENUE OF THE GIANTS • California, USA

This scenic, thirty-two-mile portion of the historic Highway 101 is located within Northern California's Humboldt Redwoods State Park, a silent and entrancing world of sky-high trees—some two thousand years old and taller than a thirty-story building. They promise what the Japanese call "forest bathing," the simple act of spending time in pristine surroundings.

IGUAZU FALLS • Argentina/Brazil

You will literally soak up the power on display at the largest waterfall system in the world, a thunderous network of hundreds of multitiered cascades that gush up to 13 million liters per second. The viewing platform lets you get daringly close to Devil's Throat, one of the most spectacular of the fourteen waterfalls.

MORAINE LAKE, BANFF NATIONAL PARK • Alberta, Canada

Kayakers head to the heart of Canada's first national park and Moraine Lake, whose brilliant blue-green color is a result of glacier-fed water. The surrounding snow-dusted peaks of the Canadian Rockies create a postcard-like scene that is almost too beautiful to imagine.

ANSE SOURCE D'ARGENT, LA DIGUE • Seychelles

This Indian Ocean beach offers an abundance of restorative beauty to visitors: white sand, palms waving in the breeze, gin-clear waters, plus scattered car-sized boulders that look like Henry Moore sculptures and give the feeling of an open-air art gallery.

THE SAND DUNES OF SOSSUSVLEI • Namibia

The epic landscapes of the Namib Desert feel otherworldly, with some of the planet's highest sand dunes, reaching one thousand feet high. Wind is forever changing their shapes, and their colors range from orange to salmon to rust to pink and are most breathtaking just after sunrise.

Facing page: Iguazu Falls, bordering Argentina and Brazil

A good guest is always welcomed back.

Algarve, Portugal

And the end of all our exploring
Will be to arrive where we started
And know the place for the first time.

—T. S. ELIOT

Acknowledgments

Eternal thanks to Peter and Carolan Workman, and to their remarkable publishing-house family, who adopted me decades ago. Without them, *1,000 Places to See Before You Die*—and this, its most recent offspring—would never have come to be. I thank them for helping to provide me with this deeply rewarding life where I get to travel the world and write about it. Yes, I do have the world's best job.

My gratitude goes to editor in chief Suzie Bolotin, who was one of the first people to ever ask me not only where I was off to next, or had just returned from, but why I traveled. It was a simple enough question whose answers she hoped would be varied, numerous, and inspiring enough to fill these pages—at the very least enough to stoke one's armchair wanderlust, and at best to propel some of you out the front door.

The first draft of this book slowly took shape under the patient guidance of my now-former editor Margot Herrera, with whom I shared decades of 1,000 Places–related brainstorming and writing, and was so perfectly finalized and finessed by Mary Ellen O'Neill, who guided it into the final stretch, with an assist from Alexis August, who helped make sense of it all.

The selection, mix, and design of the photos enlivening these pages was a truly appreciated labor of love by Anne Kerman, Lisa Hollander, and Vaughn Andrews. They must have snuck inside my brain or read every journal I've ever written to have created such a perfect accompaniment to my anecdotes and bons mots.

That's where Hillary Leary, Marta Jaremko, and Barbara Peragine stepped in and performed their age-old editorial and typesetting magic so that this beautiful specimen could shine—with Claire McKean keeping everything tightly on schedule. And thank you David Schiller for keeping your keen and discerning eye on every last thing.

Judging from past collaborations, I know the publicity and marketing team of Rebecca Carlisle, Diana Griffin, Moira Kerrigan, and Kate Oksen will do wondrous things to make sure this book gets seen by all those who share my insatiable desire to see the world.

To all of the above—and for all of the above reasons—I leave you with one thousand heartfelt thank-yous. I have no doubt you always went the extra mile.

Photo Credits